The Reality of
Fighting

The Reality of
Fighting

A straight-forward look at the
Martial Arts and the truth about
fighting in the real world.

RJ Defaye

Library of Congress Control Number:		2011901946
ISBN:	Hardcover	978-1-4568-5444-7
	Softcover	978-1-4568-5443-0
	Ebook	978-1-4568-4404-2

This is a work of fiction. Names, characters, places and incidents either are the product of the author's imagination or are used fictitiously, and any resemblance to any actual persons, living or dead, events, or locales is entirely coincidental.

This book was printed in the United States of America.

To order additional copies of this book, contact:
Xlibris Corporation
1-800-618-969
www.xlibris.com.au
Orders@xlibris.com.au
500571

CONTENTS

Why We Fight

Why shouldn't we fight? Why should fighting *always* be a last resort in a world where fighting seems to be the most effective way of getting what you want? It should be obvious to everyone with half a brain that fighting is wrong. Violence is wrong. Unfortunately, it seems that violence is the only thing that can stop violence. It is an endless cycle; it goes on and on, and it is a basic human instinct that many people find impossible to ignore. In some people, violence is ingrained in their behaviour from a young age, and they are brought up not entirely understanding the ramifications that violence can have on their lives, whereas others are brought up to ignore such violent tendencies. But you can't ignore a punch; you can't politely ask a knife to go away, and in this day and age where society no longer seems to have any morals, your politeness would only be laughed at. If you turn the other cheek, people *are* going to hit you, and they will keep hitting you all day long. Many daydreamers believe that fighting solves nothing—but I bet these people have never been backed into a corner by someone who was determined to hurt them no matter how hard they begged for mercy, nor have they ever had to fight for their lives. The only way to get out of a situation like that is to either fight or hope that the beating you are about to get is not too severe. I wish to make it clear from the very beginning that I do not enjoy violence; I despise fighting, and I am disgusted by people who have no control over their tempers and become aggressive at the drop of a hat. As you get to know a bit more about me, you may find it strange that I have such beliefs, but what you must realise is that being good at something and enjoying something can be two different things entirely.

In modern times, it seems that violence is more often than not the deciding factor in most disputes. We fight because we're forced to, but it should never be the first choice in any situation, and in an ideal world it wouldn't be. But this is not an ideal world. Turn on your television or read a newspaper and you'll understand what I mean.

Humans for all appearances seem to be the most violent species on the planet. Certainly our ability to fight on a very large scale sets us apart from the other creatures that share this world. Humans will fight for just about any reason, big and small. Love, lust, dominance, power, fortune, pride, honour, hate, greed, protection, and survival are the most common reasons that we fight each other. What really sets us apart, however, is the fact that many people fight or inflict violence and pain (and sometimes death) on others for the sheer thrill of it. I have known people who have gone out with the express purpose of getting into an altercation—just for the fun of a fight. I know a few people who will joyfully walk down the street and pick a fight with a complete stranger just for the fun of it, satisfying some sick desire to assert power over another human being. I have no interest at all in what causes this kind of behaviour, nor do I have any interest in the psychological reasons behind the behaviour of the kind of people who randomly and deliberately commit violent acts. The only thing that concerns me about this is that it happens and that highly aggressive people like this actually exist in our society. Just remember as you're reading this that there *are* people out there who love fighting and pain—they *live* for it because it excites them and in some twisted way makes them feel better about themselves. Average, sensible people try to stay away from fights, so it's the above-mentioned people who will cause you the most trouble.

The Plan and Who I Am

The purpose of this book is not to act as a martial arts manual, nor am I attempting to teach or promote any single art or way of thinking. My aim is simply to pass on the knowledge and experience I have gained throughout my life as a martial artist who has witnessed some extreme acts of violence, all of which have had a profound effect on me. Please do not mistake me for some kind of tough guy trying to big-note myself; I am simply writing this in an attempt to enlighten the average person as to the dangers of fighting, but hopefully something within these pages will also help those who find themselves in dangerous situations on a regular basis and simply cannot avoid confrontations. I also aim to briefly explore the evolution of hand-to-hand combat from its origins to today's modern fighting systems so that you may gain a better understanding of the history behind self-defence. As well as this, I will attempt to look at certain issues that you might come up against as a martial artist during your training (both as a student and a teacher), and finally I will attempt to convey my views on realistic hand-to-hand combat and why it is best to avoid getting into a fight altogether. In doing this, I am not going to attempt to overwhelm you with a lot of scientific and/or psychological jargon that, I have noticed, many martial artists seem to focus on these days, and rather than trying to calm their minds and centre themselves, they fill their heads with confusion and dull their basic senses which are vital to their protecting themselves in dangerous situations. The main aim of this book is to act as a starting point from which you may gain ideas about doing your own research in new martial arts, rather than attempt to write everything there is to know about martial arts and take up thousands of pages.

Now who am I? I am nobody special. I'm not the greatest fighter who has ever lived, I can't destroy groups of armed attackers with ease, I have never won any awards, and I've never been in any movies or magazines; that is simply not why I became a martial artist. Martial arts is to me like breathing; I have been doing it as long I can remember, and it is such a large part of my life that I could never stop doing it for long. My interest in the martial arts started when I was around four or five as my elder brother was a member of the local karate club, and I used to mimic whatever he did when he was training in the yard at home until eventually I was allowed to start going to the classes myself. It has been quite a journey since then, studying several other martial arts such as hapkido, Brazilian ju-jitsu, Muay

Thai, boxing, Tae Kwon Do, Kung Fu, several styles of karate, as well as military close combat and weapons systems.

As a kid growing up in the 1980s and 1990s, I was heavily influenced at the time by the movies that Hollywood was churning out concerning the martial arts. Back then all I remember wanting to be was a high flying spin-kick throwing hero who always gets the bad guys. But even though my motivations have changed, my enthusiasm has not been dulled in the least. As I grew up, so did my love for the martial arts, and in turn I gained more and more knowledge, but it wasn't until my days in an all-boys Sydney high school that I really started learning. Besides what many might think about all-boys schools and the many jokes that go flying around about the subject, I can assure you that it was quite the opposite, and because there were around 1500 of us and no females except for some of the teachers, everyone was trying to prove their manhood in the most male way possible. It was not a pleasant environment at all. Testosterone levels were through the roof, and because our school was part of a major sporting network of schools there were a great deal of large, fit, and highly aggressive young men around all too willing to beat the crap out of each other just so they could prove to their friends that they were cool. Very rarely did I go a day without seeing at least one brawl in the yard or on the fields or behind the buildings, and because of this you either stood up or you sat in the corner and minded your own business, pretending to be invisible. I put a lot of martial arts theory into practice when I was at that school (for six years, mind you) even though at the time I was too immature to understand how dangerous my actions were. However, this was nothing compared to what lay ahead for me when I became an adult.

After I finished school and started at university, I found myself in a few street scuffles, mostly because I was sticking my nose in where it didn't belong and because I was in a new town. However, it wasn't until I started working as a bouncer that I began to be involved in and witnessed some extreme and horrific situations, and in many cases I would have to put to the test many of the things that I had been taught. I learnt a lot of painful truths during that time.

The humble bouncer gets a bad rap these days. They are stereotyped into being angry steroid freaks with very low IQ's and a single minded desire to beat people up, but I found for the most part that the opposite was true. Although there are still some thugs within the industry, I found the majority of my workmates to be caring, generous, and articulate individuals who were lured by the call of easy money (which unless you are involved in an altercation this is true). I would not trade my time with them for any amount of money. I also met a lot of other colourful people during that time: martial arts champions, ex special forces types, highly experienced brawlers, drug dealers/users, members of organised crime gangs, motorcycle gang members, and some first-rate lunatics. Some of the things I witnessed during that time had a profound effect on me in both good and bad ways. For a long time, I had nightmares and felt physically ill when remembering some of the things that I had seen happen, but once I had gotten over my initial shock of the violence I began to open my eyes to the fact that many of the things that I had learnt throughout my training had to be re-thought and perhaps put to the test. The experiment began. I figured that since I had put myself in this situation I was going to make the most of it and hopefully come out a better person—if I came out at all.

During my time both on the streets and working in clubs, I've seen just about everything from a harmless bit of push and shove to a full-on biker brawl and beyond. I've been forced to defend myself both inside and outside of work from fists, bottles, sticks, chairs, poles, knives, and even high-heeled shoes (girls can be nasty too). I've been spat on, bled on, urinated on, and thrown up on—all deliberately. If it weren't for my training, I believe that I would have been in serious trouble more times than I could count.

Probably the biggest lesson I've learned from these experiences and the martial arts is to never take anything at face value. There are a lot of people out there who promote various things as 'street wise', 'the best way to defeat your opponent' or even statements as bold as 'in three hours learn eight moves that will make you invincible against any attacker'. Yeah. Seriously. Don't *ever* blindly follow anything or anyone. Make sure that you always question everything; even if you appear annoying by asking too many questions, it is better to ask continuously than to blindly follow something that may in the long term cause you some serious damage.

There is always going to be different opinions concerning just about everything in life, and the martial arts are no different. Take for instance the fact that Tae Kwon Do practitioners and Muay Thai practitioners throw their kicks in very different ways. The kicks are essentially the same movement, but they are executed in such a way as to make them unique to that particular style. The hardcore practitioners of each system believe that their way of executing a certain technique is the correct way, and many of them (though obviously not all) will simply refuse to even consider a different possibility, and rather than simply accept the idea that there may be a way of doing something that is just as efficient, if not more so, they completely reject the idea altogether. To me, that is not the spirit of the martial arts, and it goes against everything that I believe a martial artist should be. You should always be open to new ideas and search for something that might make you all the more efficient in your studies.

An old karate sensei of mine once wrote down a short passage for me. I do not know where it came from, and it may well be his personal philosophy. Whatever its origin, I consider it to be the most accurate description of the way a martial artist should think and behave:

It is my opinion that a student of the Martial Arts must develop their own form of physical, mental, and spiritual expression. One is not simply a student of Karate, Kung Fu, Tae Kwon Do etc. One is a student of the interpretation of their art. Therefore, in essence, they are student, teacher, and master all in one. Each participant leaves their own stamp on their chosen field. Much as the painter causes his audience to ponder the significance of a single line of colour within his masterpiece—so does the student of boxing cause the judoka to stare in wonder when he witnesses the boxer's skill for the first time. When an element from one world is introduced to another world, the latter is irreversibly changed. This is the nature of the true martial arts. This is the nature of life. Add a little something extra to your meal and it may taste all the better.

It is my hope that at least some of my knowledge and experience will in some way, shape, or form help you to either become or evolve into a smarter practitioner of the martial Arts and perhaps help you if you are ever in a sticky situation.

Evolution

Beginnings

It is widely considered that martial arts were developed in order for people to know how to better defend themselves, others, and their properties. Today, generally when we refer to the martial arts we are referring to a method that teaches you to fight by using your body as a weapon. However, this is not an entirely accurate idea as the true martial arts involve teaching and learning *all* of the different methods of warfare as well. For example, the samurai would learn a series of martial arts that were intended to prepare them for war. As well as conventional hand-to-hand and weapons training, the samurai would practice horse riding and mounted archery as a form of martial art—something that in this day and age would not be considered a form of fighting but to the samurai was incredibly important, and combining it with their other martial arts (for example, using a sword while riding a horse) made them more complete warriors. We could even go so far as to say that a soldier learning to fire his rifle is, in essence, learning a new martial art—but for simplicity's sake, I will stick to the modern interpretation.

Another important aspect of the martial arts that is often overlooked in modern society is the fact that spirituality was just as important as the physical aspect of the art. In particular, the oriental martial arts were steeped in Buddhist tradition with perhaps the most outstanding example being the Shaolin Buddhist monks who are in essence fighting priests. The monks originally practised the martial arts in order to defend the precious temple from bandits and those who sought to take what little the monks had and also to defend themselves while travelling. To this day the monks continue to practice it now with the same spirit even though they no longer need to defend it against thieves.

It is here at the Shaolin Temple that many people believe that the martial arts had their beginnings, and in a sense that is correct, even though that is not completely accurate. It is widely considered that the predecessor to what we now call the martial arts (kung fu, karate, etc.) was developed by Buddhist monks, who travelled around the known world and taught their forms of hand-to-hand combat to other monks so that they could protect themselves as they performed their duties. Perhaps the best noted case of this is the monk known as Bodhidharma, who travelled from India to the Shaolin Temple at the end of the fifth century AD and taught the monks there how to defend themselves.[1] From there, it was developed into what we now refer to as kung fu, of which there are many different styles throughout the world. From there, it spread throughout Asia influencing almost all of the oriental martial arts in some form or another.

When it comes to pointing directly to the world's very first martial art, however, the task is almost impossible. I believe that ever since there has been a need to defend oneself against something there has been some form of martial art in existence. I'm sure that in our very early history, one 'caveman' must have taught his son or his friend the best way to swing a stick or throw a rock in order to fight against something that was attacking him, and in my mind those would have been the very earliest forms of martial arts from which all the others were derived.

Historians do know for certain, however, that during the very first Olympics thousands of years ago many of the sports were combat orientated and that boxing and wrestling were among the sports that were offered. Perhaps these could be considered the very first martial arts designed for sporting purposes, but as for the very first organised martial arts, there is no conclusive evidence in my opinion.

I have many friends who are confused about the martial arts and all of the different styles that are on offer, but to rattle off names and descriptions of every style would take forever, and I suppose it *would* be confusing if you did not know a little about the history of the martial arts. In the martial arts, there are styles within styles, and each of these sub-systems were developed by students of the original art who developed their own interpretation of the techniques they were being taught. And through either being unable or unwilling to add their influence to their original system, they would design a new system of fighting mostly based around their parent system, but with

---

[1]   While doing research, this was the most common story I came across although there are other tales floating around.

their own personal touches and slight differences. For example, there are countless styles of karate around the world, all of which have ties back to the few original arts that developed in Okinawa (a small island south of Japan), which in turn has ties to Chinese kung fu, which in turn has ties to the Buddhist monks who taught it at the Shaolin temple (which may in turn have links to the 'caveman' I mentioned before). It is the evolution of the martial arts world, and it is continuing to evolve today.

Bruce Lee—The Ultimate Realist

It would be remiss of me if I was to talk about the evolution and realities of the martial arts and not mention perhaps the most important person in its modern history. Bruce Lee is a household name throughout the world. He is a pop-culture reference and is famous for his movies and his incredible fighting ability. However, many people including many martial artists still do not fully understand what he was about. Perhaps trying to understand his views is not really the point as it is our interpretation of his views that is perhaps more important. Bruce was the fighter's fighter, the truth seeker, and the ultimate myth buster. During perhaps his most influential years (1960s and early 1970s until his death in 1973), Bruce paved the way for the creation of the more modern martial arts of today. As he stated in TV interviews and in his writings, he did not simply practise and teach one specific style. Towards the end of his time, he did not promote any style or system even though the roots of his fighting method were based in Wing Chun Kung Fu and a style called Jun Fan Gung Fu (a style he created). What he did do was promote the concept which he called jeet kune do (the way of the intercepting fist). Bruce was essentially the first modern cross-trainer. He would devour as much information as possible regarding as many arts as he could come across and then teach his students everything he had learned, even from more obscure fighting styles at the time such as French savate. From there, he would encourage his students to find out which techniques worked best for them and practise their own interpretation of the martial arts, using his jeet kune do philosophy as the basis for their own styles. Essentially, therefore, two practitioners of jeet kune do could have completely different styles of fighting whereas students of traditional systems would have similar fighting styles.

In his teachings, he would emphasise the idea of absorbing what was useful and rejecting what was useless for one as an individual fighter, urging his students not to stick to simply one form of art but to explore all arts in the hope of refining and improving their own interpretations of the martial arts.

A passage from the Tao of jeet kune do reads:

> *Stylists, instead of looking directly into the fact, cling to forms (theories) and go on entangling themselves further and further, finally putting themselves into an inextricable snare.*[2]

He is essentially giving a reason as to why he created jeet kune do by saying that rather than exploring and confirming what they are taught, many people who dedicate themselves to the one system of martial arts sometimes simply choose to blindly believe what they are taught as being the gospel truth and do not seek to test what they have learnt or perhaps refuse to consider that there may be a more efficient way for them to go about things. Bruce's ideas were about expanding your mind by offering hints and showing you the way that things *can* be done rather than *telling* you the way they *should* be done. He was a truly brilliant and wonderful man—the Einstein of the martial arts.

---

[2] Bruce Lee, 1975, *Tao of Jeet Kune Do* (Ohara Publications, Incorporated: Santa Clarita, California).

Modern Martial Arts

In the decades since Bruce Lee's untimely death, the martial Arts have become incredibly popular throughout the world. As with everything that is popular at one time or another, Hollywood took advantage of this massive new craze and made an incredible number of movies glorifying the martial arts throughout the 1970s, 1980s, and 1990s. However, many of these movies almost set back a lot of the good work that had been done to try and dispel a lot of the mysticism and garbage that surrounded the arts. These movies completely misrepresented the martial arts that they were attempting to glorify with the emphasis being on heavily muscled heroes performing high-flying kicks and 'special secret moves'. I won't name these movies, but they know who they are. As with a lot of movies at the time, it was not so much a matter of creating a correct perception of certain arts; it was more about looking cool and making money, and with this as the priority, I must say that many movie makers succeeded.

Thankfully, a lot of this nonsense has been done away with in the last ten to fifteen years by the emergence of *simulated* reality martial arts fights known as mixed martial arts fights, where participants from every style can put their knowledge to the test against each other in a safe environment (statistically safer than professional boxing) with very few limitations. Mostly held in a cage or boxing ring, these fights have all of the safety rules that you would expect from a professional sport, and although initially outlawed in most parts of the world, it has quickly spread to many countries and is now a major sport with many different versions and heroes. This form of competition was originally outlawed due to the fact that it was simply *too* realistic in that participants in some cases were allowed to strike the groin, head-butt, kick opponents while they were down, etc. From memory, I believe that the only things they weren't allowed to do were eye-gouging and hitting the throat—everything else was fair game. This drew some of the nastiest confrontations that had ever been caught on film and was simply too brutal for the governing bodies to allow to become a mainstream sport.

It seems now that the idea of cross-training in many different martial arts has become fashionable, and we now seem to be in something of a close-combat renaissance. However, like a miniature representation of the martial arts as a whole, this new craze has also gone through a major evolution. Mixed martial arts matches changed forever when a family from

Brazil brought their own unique system of fighting into the arena, and its impact was undeniable.

When the Gracie family came along with their version of ju-jitsu (Gracie ju-jitsu—a grappling—and wrestling-based scientific art), they tore apart everyone who challenged them. They were an unstoppable force within the MMA arena. The three main brothers that really made it big were Rickson, Royler, and Royce, who with their incredible skills would either twist their opponents into knots or choke them unconscious on the ground. For years, they dominated the martial arts scene, and many people abandoned their stand-up fighting in favour of this seemingly unbeatable system. But then something else happened.

In an interview in 1995, a man by the name of Dan Inosanto (Bruce Lee's top student and the only man certified by Bruce to teach jeet kune do) declared that although Brazilian ju-jitsu was dominating the martial arts at the moment he believed that there would soon be a change and that many fighters would begin combining their stand-up fighting with wrestling arts such as ju-jitsu. That is exactly what happened. It seemed that all of a sudden there were fighters coming out from everywhere, who were just as good on the ground as they were standing up, and these days there is barely a mixed martial artist who is not well versed in both styles of fighting.

Of course, MMA is not the be all and end all of martial arts. It is simply the latest evolution of the fighting and competitive combat arts. It is my belief that it is within the military that you will find the most unrestrained forms of martial arts doing what they were originally designed to do—defend and kill. At around the time of the Second World War some militaries began to teach martial arts to certain units, but those were largely unaltered and identical to what civilians could learn. Eventually, those martial arts were modified to suit the requirements of the militaries, and even brand new fighting methods were created aimed directly at military or law enforcement use. Arts like Krav Maga (Israeli), MCMAP (Marine Corp Martial Arts Program—USA), and military Sambo (Russian) are perhaps the ultimate in realistic and practical self-defence training in modern times. I came to this conclusion because, having studied both mainstream martial arts and the military styles, I noticed that there was a vast difference between the two. For some reason, the mainstream, for the most part, does not teach the art as it was originally intended, whereas the military arts are aimed at pure realism and application in combat. The military martial arts do away with the spirituality and the long hours of dedicated practice to master single moves and instead teach the most simple, direct, and effective ways of dealing with an enemy. One could argue that, in effect, they take the art out of the martial art and break it down to its purest form (which is not necessarily a good thing due to the fact that you are taught the techniques but not the self-discipline to use them only in defence).

Becoming a Martial Artist

Learning

I've been asked from time to time by people who are interested in practicing some form of martial art about which art I think they should do, thinking perhaps that one art is inherently better than another. Mostly the answer to this question is that anything is better than nothing. Of course, that really isn't a satisfactory answer, and obviously I have my own opinions as to what does and doesn't work, but it all boils down to what you want to gain from your training. Some people want to do it for competition or something along those lines, which is fine, and other people just want to build up their confidence a little and get fit which is another good reason, but I think those priorities need to be figured out before you choose which martial art you want to do. For example, becoming a student of proper ninjutsu is not going to be any good if you want to go to tournaments, but it will do wonders for your flexibility, confidence, fitness, and ability to defend yourself. One thing I am bothered by is that sometimes people's priorities change, but their training does not. For instance, a classic example is of people who have been training purely for self-defence, who decide that they want to step into the ring, but they do not change their training methods or do any research and then they wonder why their fights go so badly. As priorities change so should training.

Also as I've been stressing throughout the majority of this book, for a serious martial artist it is not so much important what art you do; it's how you make it work and whether or not you explore the truths behind it and whether or not you are willing to try and learn from everything you come across. You must also try to come to understand through experience the difference between the artistic value of a certain style and rubbish that is trying to pawn itself off as a legitimate art form or system of defence.

I've certainly been to a few schools where the stuff I was learning, in my opinion, was an absolute joke. But without having done that, I would never have completely realised exactly who were and who weren't good-quality instructors.

Now, on the other hand, there *is* such a thing as a bad student—no matter what anyone says. One thing that I absolutely cannot stand are students who come to a class, pay their money to take part in the class, and then do nothing but complain the entire time about it being too hard and that they're not any good at it and they don't want to do it any more. Why the hell do these people bother coming to the class and wasting their damn money? It is rude and it disrupts the other people who are actually trying to learn. I had a friend who wanted me to teach her boxing, but all she did for the entire lesson (which was free, mind you) was go back and forward getting glasses of water and complaining that she was too uncoordinated. 'Damn it! I'm trying to teach you how to be more coordinated!' I never taught her again after that, but she still to this day claims that she knows how to box.

This brings me to another thing that you should try to avoid as a student; arrogant tendencies. In modern times, a lot of the spirituality has gone out of the martial arts, and this is breeding a culture of students who love nothing more than using their skills on innocent people. I remember a first Dan karate black belt who was so full of himself that he would go to other schools and challenge the instructors at those schools. Most of the instructors told him to go away, but one young teacher took him up on his challenge and within five seconds the challenger was knocked out cold and the instructor went back to teaching his class. Essentially, there are a lot more highly trained thugs out there than there used to be. They should be ashamed of themselves. When you become a martial artist, you take on a great number of skills that give you a physical advantage over other people. The problem is that these days nobody teaches their students to use their skills responsibly. It wasn't really that long ago that people were still being taught to use these skills in self-defence only, was it? Perhaps I'm just getting old. When I was working as a bouncer, I saw highly trained thugs everywhere, and I have to admit that it was intimidating. The good guys weren't the only ones with the skills any more. It was a sad thing to notice, but I guess it's a reflection of the times we live in now—good guys don't always win the day any more.

Moving on, I also feel that I need to point out to anyone who is new to the martial arts that there is a very large difference between sport and self-defence. I feel I must do this for your safety and my own peace of mind because I have seen all too many instances of the champions in the ring getting their teeth handed to them by an experienced and aggressive street fighter. I'm not trying to put down any arts or upset anyone; I'm just being as truthful as possible because in a class everything is pretty and perfect and even when sparring everything almost turns out like the fights you see in the movies, but real fights are rarely as pretty. In fact, in a real fight it's all you can do to land *one* clean shot on the other person/people.

I have trained with a lot of people in a lot of different styles, and I have noticed a lot of things that are different in the sports world compared to the self-defence styles that I mainly studied in. For example, I had a friend when I went to university whose name was Dale, and man was he cool! We hit it off straight away when I caught him reading a martial arts magazine one day, and we both realised that we had a great deal in common. He had trained in the style of Tae Kwon Do that they currently use in the Olympics and he had even sparred with one of the guys from the Olympic team, whom he had met through a friend. Every time we trained together, we would end up sparring and he would kick the hell out of me, showing me what I was doing wrong with some of my kicks and how to get the most speed out of certain positions. The problem was, however, that this was a completely different style from what I was used to. We would stand with our hands already up and we would be two metres apart before he would call out for the spar to begin (with light contact and competition rules). Well, I was hobbled from the start. I wasn't allowed to hit hard or grapple, nor was I allowed to use joint, throat, eye, or groin strikes (not that I would want to use such moves on my friend, however). He eliminated almost all of my go-to moves (techniques that are favoured and committed to muscle memory). However, whenever I tried to teach Dale anything, he would shrug it off and insist that I was the one who needed more lessons because he was the one who always kicked the hell out of me in sparring. It made my blood boil for a little while, but I got over it; we were friends, so what else could I do? Maybe I should have made a better attempt at gaining his attention. I could have tried harder even if in the end it made no difference. I could have at least tried. Dale and I were drinking at a certain night-time hot spot (one which in later years I would actually work at) and I was on the dance floor while Dale was getting us some more drinks. I looked over to see what was taking him so long when I noticed that he was involved in an argument where both he and the other guy were inches away from each other's face. It happened so fast that it's hard to remember how it exactly went down, but I do remember Dale being head-butted and then stomped on by three people while he was unconscious on the ground. Trying to help my friend only resulted in me being restrained by security and led out with the rest of the guys involved. Dale, however, left in an ambulance. I saw him a few times while he was in hospital (which was approximately a week), but after that he went home to his parents in Melbourne and I never saw him again, and my phone calls and emails went unanswered. Maybe he just wanted to forget that the entire thing ever happened. I don't know.

The point that I am trying to get at is that a lot of the things that I wanted to show Dale were things that were out of his comfort zone, for example, why not to be inches away from the face of someone who is angry with you (obviously because you're at risk of a head-butt). To me it was common sense, and I am in no way trying to say that my friend was some kind of idiot. I am simply trying to imply that although he was good at the type of training that he had always done, he had never bothered to gain any experience out of his comfort zone and was therefore not ready for an attack which I saw coming from a mile away. To know the difference between training for a sport and training for self-defence and not allowing yourself, as a student, to be led astray by misguided teachers is a step in the right direction. If you want your sport training to be handy in the street as well, then perhaps drill it in realistic scenarios and not constantly in a sporting environment, like I did with my friend Dale. Take the pads off (except mouth guards), wear normal clothes instead of whatever uniforms you wear to class, and learn how you react to things when you don't know they're coming. Learn how your body naturally reacts so that you can be ready for your own automatic responses.

Now moving on to perhaps a more obscure method of learning, there has been a fair bit of argument and controversy over the years about the benefits of learning from books and films. The truth is that they are an essential source of information, but they are no substitute for a good instructor and training partner. I have found, however, that the more highly trained you are, the easier it is to gain very useful knowledge from these sources. If all you need is a push in the right direction, then they are just the ticket. When I first began my research into military close combat and knife combat, a friend of mine put me on to some videos made by a man called Mike Lee Kanarek, who teaches an Israeli system of martial arts which is battle tested and proven, known as Haganah.[3] This really gave

---

[3]   www.fight2survive.com

me good ideas about what I should be looking for in military and realistic self-defence.

However, I have also known some complete morons who have read a few karate books from cover to cover and have then gone around telling people that they are black belts. Some of them have even gone on to teach people what they 'know'—people who simply don't know any better because they have not had much exposure to the martial arts. One of those so-called teachers was a guy we nicknamed 'Dodgy Roger'. Now Roger had seen one too many movies and had read one too many books, and after taking a couple of karate classes, he thought himself capable of teaching others how to defend themselves. He would walk around with fake trophies that he had supposedly won in some big tournament, and the reason why we never saw him with any training injuries was because he was 'just that good' and the reason that we never heard of these tournaments was because they were supposedly illegal underground bare-knuckle fights that only a select few people knew about. In reality, Roger knew almost nothing, and he caused more than a few dangerous situations with his showboating and eventually we set him straight. Be careful of people who talk too much about their martial prowess and how often they train because nine times out of ten those people are not who they claim to be. Going back to the original point, learning from books and videos can be an invaluable resource, but don't make the mistake of turning into our friend Roger and thinking that watching a few tapes and reading a few books makes you an expert.

Also, as a final note on the subject, watch out for older texts and films because many of them do not promote very safe practices. In such cases, you should use your common sense or ask someone with the appropriate knowledge.

Teaching

To start with, and this is going to sound arrogant, and it is in relation to the story about my friend Dale, if you've never been in a *real* self-defence situation and never *honestly* had your physical well-being threatened, then you have absolutely no business teaching anything directly aimed at self-defence or promoting anything of that nature. That's not to say that you shouldn't be teaching martial arts at all. What I'm saying is that if you've never done it, then you cannot teach others how to do it. It would be the same if I tried to train someone for a fight in a boxing ring—I have absolutely no experience fighting in the ring and I have no right to try and teach anyone how to do it because it is a completely different game from what I am used to. That is also not to say that you should go out right now and start a fight and see if all of the stuff that you have learned actually does work. It is just my truthful opinion that if you want to teach realistic self-defence you should have some experience. It may seem unfair to say something like that, but it is also unfair to your students for you to be teaching something that you have no experience in. Remember, teaching martial arts (of any kind at all) is a completely different thing from teaching self-defence, even though the two are undeniably related. Many of the best self-defence experts and fighters come from career backgrounds that allow for the practical application of martial arts techniques such as military, law enforcement, and security (private or general). When learning from such people, you can really tell the difference as opposed to someone who has simply been taught and is in turn teaching and has never practically applied their knowledge in appropriate situations. The same is true when learning to drive a car in that you don't sit down and have someone tell you how to drive a car when they've never driven one before. Instead you find someone who has been driving for a long time and you get them to teach you and so on.

This brings me to another point when it comes to teaching martial arts. As a teacher you have a great responsibility to your students. You are teaching them a set of life skills, skills they will live by and may perhaps depend on for survival. If a student asks a question, no matter how stupid it may seem to you, you must make sure that the student gets the best answer you can give them even if it's 'I'm not sure. Let's work it out together'. You must also ensure that your students are competent in their techniques *before* they advance in level.

For many years now, there has been a very irritating trend for schools to simply hand out ranks to students who have not earned them. These schools charge large membership and lesson fees and then charge another large fee when the students go for their level grading, and as long as everything is paid up, they are simply given their belts after a small demonstration of the things they have learned, whether they perform well or not. Schools of this nature are known as 'McDojos': expensive but fast and easy. I know of one particular case where a person with no prior martial arts knowledge was graded to a black belt within a year. One year! If you run one of these types of schools, you need to have a good hard look at what you are doing to yourself, your students, and the martial arts in general. Certainly if you teach at a full-time Dojo and it's your only source of income you want to keep your students happy, but at what cost? Do you really think allowing students with inferior skills to pass their tests just so that you can keep their business is really fair to them, the art, or even yourself?

Teaching in a class full of students can be a lot of fun, and it is the preferred method in modern society (in the West at least). However, I find that teaching in the same way that the old-timers did (one on one or in a very small group) is a much more rewarding experience for both the student and the teacher. It allows the instructor to figure out the best way to run the class for that particular student in order to focus on what they need to work on, and it allows for strong bonds to be formed between the student and the teacher. I've had some students who love to just drill until they have no energy left and they're covered with sweat, but on the other hand, I've had students who prefer to dissect moves and take things much slower so that they can properly focus on the actual technique. In a class full of different people, achieving something like this is very hard, and most people will simply not get the type of training that they need and sadly some of those people give the martial arts away because they think in some way that it is their fault that they are not learning as quickly as the other people. Also, I don't wear uniforms and I don't charge money, but much like the teachers of old, I get to know my students before I teach them anything. I simply do not want to teach someone who I believe will use my techniques in an irresponsible manner. However, if you are running a Dojo or a gym, there are going to obviously be expenses that need to be considered because after all business is business.

Training

Now everyone trains in their own way, but I feel that I have to express a grave concern that I have about many schools out there—that they are perhaps not training their students in a correct manner. Again, this is simply my humble opinion, but I feel that it has to be said. I'll start with an example. I once went to a new Dojo, back when I trained in groups, and the instructor was a very nice guy. However, I noticed that after the initial warm-up period the class consisted of about 80 per cent fitness and 20 per cent actual martial arts training. As at the time I was a bodybuilder, I didn't want to jeopardise my weight workouts by doing anything that might interrupt the healing time that I had to give my muscles (I treated the martial arts classes more like relaxation time and a chance for a little bit of cardio activity to supplement the weightlifting). I let it slide for a little while, thinking that perhaps this was not a usual night for this particular school, but after five classes nothing had changed, and the entire two-hour session was a gruelling workout as my body was already sore from my daily trips to the gym, and I found that I was not learning very much in the way of the actual technique.

This led to me actually approaching the instructor and asking him if we could perhaps do more martial arts work and less fitness work. After all, I was not paying to learn how to do push-ups; I already knew how to do them quite well and I didn't need any further instruction on that subject. I was getting a little annoyed by this stage. He responded by saying that the workouts made the students more able to perform the martial arts that they were being taught. This was a valid point apart from the fact that once the workouts were over the students were too exhausted to perform the techniques properly and instead executed a sloppy technique which he did not seem to correct whatsoever. He also said to me that he was busy outside of the dojo and did not have time to do his own workouts and this is what he preferred to do.

That statement infuriated me, and from there an argument ensued in which I was asked to leave, which I did immediately. The idea of a teacher using the time that is supposed to be set aside for his students is appalling to me. It appeared to me that they were paying for him to do his workout to the detriment of their actual learning. Sure, it's fine to put your students through a warm-up and maybe a few push-ups to loosen the joints etc., but to make the warm-up last for most of the class is an absolute waste of time.

Even professional fighters these days distinguish between their workouts and their actual technique training, and the way I see it, if all they wanted to do was get fit the students of that school would have joined a gym instead of going to a martial arts class. Perhaps I was out of line, but I stand by my point of view and I make no apologies.

Also, when you are training, you must make sure that you are in a safe environment and that what you are doing could not possibly be detrimental to your health. Of course, I'm not talking about sparring because that is an essential part of learning any martial art and can be easily controlled. I'm talking about not being reckless and perhaps going overboard when you are training. I've seen many training partners lose their professionalism and go hell for leather trying to beat the crap out of each other, which is an absolute waste of time when you are trying to train. What's the point of getting so destroyed at training that you are unable to continue for a month? You must also research everything you do and test whether or not it could be harmful. For example, there are many stretches out there that teachers insist on their students doing, but some are outdated and are actually bad for the joints. Also I had one karate instructor who insisted on making us do push-ups on the *back* of our hands. This made our hands go in the same position as many wrist locks (in particular, a lock known as the *goose-neck*) would put us in, and maybe the idea was to make our wrists tougher and perhaps immune to those types of locks, but it was dangerous and reckless and could have easily resulted in one of us breaking our wrists if we actually tried. I would also like to note that nobody ever gained the ability to do even one full push-up by attempting that method as it was impossible to get the muscles in our arms to cooperate with the odd angles. I think that's the point of the wrist locks as well.

Essentially, your training will boil down to your specific needs and what you want to gain out of it. Much as in any form of physical activity that someone may want to be better at, the training must reflect the activity. For example, when I became a bouncer I needed to gain a lot of size and become a lot stronger because my martial arts ability was not going to be enough in the sense that I was restricted in the number of moves I could perform on people due to laws concerning security licensing. Obviously my more aggressive self-defence moves had been taken out of the equation (throat shots, eye shots, etc.), so a lot of the things I had to do would be focused on wrestling, and extra strength would make that a lot easier. This caused me to start weightlifting and essentially go from 90-something kilograms to 120-something kilograms due to the specific focus in my training. I also began to concentrate less on my striking ability and more on my wrestling and lock techniques. This would be in stark contrast, for example, to anyone who was aiming at entering the ring as a boxer. Their focus would be on cardiovascular fitness and punching power (with their techniques being only clean boxing moves so as not to accidentally employ any dirty boxing in the ring), and they would do their best to not gain or lose too much weight (unless they needed to get into a different weight division)

The problem with a lot of training is that most of the time you do not get to pick and choose what you want to do. For instance, if you are a beginner standing in a class and you have had absolutely no training beforehand, then you essentially have no choice as to what you want to initially learn. At that stage, when you start learning martial arts, you have to take any and all training that is available to you; it is just a matter of fact. However, when you advance in levels and start learning new arts and gain more and more contacts within the martial arts community, you are more readily able to explore your skills than when you first started. It is at that time that many good fighters become great, and they truly start to develop their own interpretations of the martial arts. So when you start training for the first time, don't be too disheartened that you are not going exactly in the direction that you want. Take what you can from what you are learning right now and use it later on to enhance the exploration of the martial arts that you really want to focus on. Take what is useful and reject what is useless for you.

Perhaps one of the most important aspects of training is solo training. In an environment where you are all alone, you may feel more comfortable attempting moves that you are not so confident with and do not often attempt in a group environment for fear of embarrassment. I remember when I was learning spinning techniques for the first time I simply could not manage to do them correctly, and more often than not I would fall on my backside, much to the amusement of many of the other students who found those moves easier to execute than I did. Rather than give up, I turned to solo training and made myself repeat the moves over and over again until I had them at a decent level. I did not have to put up with constant ribbings from other students (and less helpful junior instructors), and I could concentrate on what I had to do. Also, in this setting, I believe it is easier to develop your signature moves because, more often than not, you are working the techniques that you find more interesting, whereas in a class setting you are working on whatever the instructor tells you to. I cannot stress enough the importance of taking what you learn and moulding it into your own fighting style, rather than remaining stagnant and doing everything the same way as everyone else, which leads to predictability and stunts your development as a fighter.

One thing that I keep hearing over and over again throughout the martial arts community (people, magazines, books, television, movies, etc.) is that fitness is an integral part of being a martial artist. I'm not so sure. Certainly being fit and healthy is beneficial to everyone no matter what they do, but is it *really* an integral part of being a martial artist? I have had many friends over the years who have supplemented their martial arts with all sorts of workout regimens such as weightlifting and running, and although they became very fit and muscular, I can't really say that this made them better fighters. Obviously, someone who is involved in martial sports needs to be fit because they are in a competitive environment and fitness will help them get through the hours and days of competition, but most of the really superb street fighters I have met during my time have all been 'average Joes'—some you might even think to perhaps be a little on the chubby side. Those are the people who have actual practical knowledge of fighting and have spent years developing their skills without ever having the need to bench press ridiculous amounts of weight or being able to run for miles without getting winded.

When everything is said and done, however, it is really up to you whether or not you want to become ultra-fit or just remain as you are, and even though learning and drilling martial art techniques will increase your fitness to a certain degree, your fitness (in my opinion) does not indicate how effective you are as a martial artist or a fighter.

Weapons

When people think about martial arts and weapons, they generally think of the weapons most used in films such as the nunchaku or katana (samurai sword). They do not generally consider the humble house key as a weapon with devastating capability. Sadly, weapons are an often overlooked aspect of martial arts training as many believe that in the age of firearms there is very little need for learning how to use a sword or a staff.

Unfortunately, until a few years ago, this was my attitude as well, and I was due for a rude awakening. Everything changed for me when one day I was at home and an incredibly dangerous situation erupted outside. My wife was at work and I had the day off, so I was sitting down and watching television when outside I heard what I thought to be some kind of domestic dispute going on right outside my window. As it turned out, it was my neighbour being beaten up by several low life individuals (numbering around 6-10) who lived at the other end of the street. It turned out that my neighbour and his girlfriend had been walking home when those other people had called out a derogatory comment to the latter, to which my neighbour took offence and initiated an argument, which led to a brawl (or more accurately a bashing). Somehow it had made its way up the street and was now happening in our driveway, but with the help of a few other neighbours, we were able to get the attackers back down the other end of the street. The police were called, but they were of very little help because the original assailants were nowhere to be seen, and when the police left it was the beginning of one of the tensest nights of my life.

Now we were all targets, rather than just my neighbour and his girlfriend, and we had to stay vigilant the entire night—we were all fair game as far as those guys were concerned. They came down the street a short time later, taunting us and informing us that they intended to rape our women, and aiming at one specific person, they said that they were going to throw his newborn baby into a fire. They then went back down the street, obviously intending to get ready for a fight. I immediately rang my wife and told her to stay at her mother's place and then rang one of my brothers, who came over as quickly as possible.

They came back at around midnight. There was now around twenty of them, and they were all armed with metal poles and pieces of wood. My brother and I were armed with simple things like baseball bats, and several other neighbours came out armed with similar objects. There were now five of us against twenty or so, and I thought I was minutes away from death—it was one of the worst feelings of my life. That feeling was made even worse when I realised that I had no idea how to effectively use a weapon in a fight. All I could think of was swinging it around wildly, and I realised that that would probably not be enough. I thought to myself that I shouldn't have wasted all of the opportunities that I'd had to learn weapon arts. I'd had plenty of invitations to learn Kobudo, Kendo, Kumdo, and even some Ninjutsu weaponry, but I had passed them all up to focus on other things that I was already good at. I think there's a time in every martial artist's life when he gets to a stage where he becomes so good at what he does that he is afraid of looking like a beginner again, and I think deep down it was that arrogance that stopped me from moving forward with that sort of training—and I thought I was going to pay dearly for my mistake. You always hear stories about people in dangerous situations and their entire life 'flashing before their eyes', but you never really understand what they mean until the same thing happens to you. As it turned out, however, just as things looked like they were going to end badly, the police turned up and all of the people scattered. The police turned up in force, and many of the houses that those people occupied were raided. Over the next few days, many of them were arrested on drug charges and previous offences. We had absolutely no idea who or what those people were, and we had almost ended up as the next victims of some very hardened criminals. I had never felt more helpless in my life. It is a horrible feeling, and for many people it is the feeling of helplessness that drives them to learn some form of martial art in order to regain a measure of the confidence lost from a certain incident. Before this event, I had a fair amount of confidence in myself as a fighter, but this was a wake-up call that I desperately needed and I now consider my weapons training to be just as important as my unarmed training.

At the time, I had reasoned that my hand-to-hand skills were good enough to hold off the average attacker, maybe even two of them at once if they weren't armed, but in my arrogance I had led myself to believe that I was capable of handling any situation. My weapons training began the next week, and since that time I have studied European sword arts, short range edged and blunt weapons, throwing weapons, and knife fighting—all of which I have blended into my own methods of fighting based on other research. Many of the skills that I have learned during this period can be directly applied to objects not often associated with weapons (such as bats and keys). These days, many people are practising arts which revolve around weapons that are commonly found in today's society—much like the Okinawans did when they were conquered by Japan. The Japanese denied the Okinawan people the right to carry any form of weapon in public and denied them the right to even own such weapons. This led to some Okinawan masters developing systems of fighting based upon simple farming equipment and staves. In modern society, many self-defence classes teach people to use their car keys, phones, books, and even dirt as weapons to either eliminate or disable their attacker. Unlike the good old wild West or colonial days, we are no longer allowed to go around openly carrying weapons to give the impression that we are *not* to be messed with. So many modern martial arts and military self-defence instructors are now teaching the concept of improvised weapons. I strongly recommend that every student of the martial arts invest some time into learning to quickly identify and use a potential improvised weapon. You will end up feeling a lot more comfortable in certain environments that you might not have had an easy time in previously once you learn to spot potential tools of self-defence. For example, you would be able to use a lot of the same moves with a baseball bat that you would with a sword of some description (if you were a student of sword fighting but didn't have a sword handy at the time and had to improvise). Obviously, a bat would not cut like a sword, but the basic principles are solid, and getting hit with a heavy blunt object still hurts a lot, trust me. The military martial art I mentioned before, Krav Maga, actually teaches its students to use 'weapons similar to . . .'. For example, it will teach you to use, among other things, a weapon similar to a stick (branches, crowbars, hammers, flash lights/torches, etc.) and teach you a series of techniques that can be applied to all of those improvised weapons. It's actually a quite exciting concept.

Weapons really are the great equaliser when it comes to combat. In essence, size counts for almost nothing, and skill is the main determining factor. A large untrained man with a tire iron can easily be brought down by a small trained man with a similar weapon, and even if the two were to be more evenly matched in training, I have noticed that most of the time bigger people have the disadvantage due to the fact that they pose a much larger target and are generally somewhat slower than smaller people. For example, I have found it difficult in a lot of my training in recent years when matched up against smaller opponents because at six feet and one inch tall and 120 or so kilograms I cannot match the speed of someone five or six inches smaller and perhaps fifty or sixty kilograms lighter than me. Normally, this wouldn't matter so much because I would have the advantage of strength, but it means next to nothing when we are doing knife simulations and I am constantly getting 'cut' because the little bugger is dancing around me like some kind of fairy. It can get irritating when your training does not go to your liking, but it all leads towards personal development where your strategies against different types of people are formulated—after all, personal development is the goal of all training; if you did everything perfect every time, you would never learn anything new.

Also, as a final note on smaller opponents, most often you will find that a small man is a lot more aggressive if he has a weapon of some kind—a scene that is commonly witnessed in many gangs that are mostly made up of teenagers, some of whom may have knives or something similar.

Just about every culture throughout history, as with hand-to-hand martial arts, has some form of weapon-based system of combat. This is especially prominent with cultures that were large enough to form nations and have armies such as Greece, Rome, the Middle East, Europe, and most Asian countries. Also, interestingly, Native Americans have quite complex systems of weapons combat that were taught to their warriors. However, as with most martial arts, it is the oriental arts that seem to be the most popular, at least in modern times anyway. Weapon-focused systems like Iaido, Kendo, Kali, and Ninjutsu (although Ninjutsu is an all-encompassing style and not simply a weapons-combat-focused art) are perhaps the most influential weapon arts on an international level as a result of either their artistic benefit or their shear realistic brutality. As with hand-to-hand martial arts, there are really no bad systems out there involving weapons; there are only bad instructors, and when you're dealing with weapons you want a professional instructor who will be concerned first and foremost with your safety. Weapons are a lot less forgiving than fists and feet. Again, trust me. Always use caution and research your systems thoroughly, and if at any time you think that you are being taken for a ride and not necessarily gaining a worthwhile education from the person teaching you, then simply walk away and find something else.

Realities

Take a Seat, Sunshine

Now this is the part of the book that may well be one of the most important things that you will read as a martial artist or even as just a regular untrained person. *Real* fights, *real* self-defence is *never ever* portrayed accurately in the movies. Never! For example, the way Bruce Lee fought in his movies is nothing like the way he really fought when he was defending himself—but he simply understood that he had to make the action in his movies more attractive for the audiences, so he threw in the flashy moves that everyone loves and that looked good on camera. In fact, it was not until Bruce Lee and Chuck Norris became associated with each other that Bruce learned the effectiveness of kicking above the waist as before this time Bruce considered that the only targets worth kicking were below the waist.

As an example of how movies and television have misrepresented martial arts and fighting in general, one might consider that in reality you cannot get broken ribs and fight as if nothing happened, and the same goes for being stabbed and shot. These things really hurt and they short-circuit your brain, taking your focus away from your skills and decreasing your ability to fight effectively. When your ribs are broken, the slightest movement or jolt hurts like hell, and forget about taking a deep breath because depending on how badly your ribs are broken you might even have a hard time talking. Now I haven't been stabbed and I've certainly never been shot, so it would be unfair for me to comment on these things and pretend that I know what I'm talking about, but having spoken to people who *have* experienced these things, it sounds as though both experiences are two of the most frightening and painful things that any person could possibly go through.

What many people, especially young men, have to understand is that fighting is not pretty, it is not glorious, it should *never* be fun, and in a real fight it is all you can do to land a clean hit on someone in the swirl and confusion of a brawl. Also sport fighting in all of its forms—even mixed martial arts and cage fights—is a completely different thing from real street fights. As soon as you introduce rules to any situation, it stops being a fight and becomes a spectacle. Just think about it; you've got gloves on. There are rules, there are people cheering, there are bets placed, and you stand there and bash each other for a prolonged period of time. In reality, an attacker won't really mind if he takes a few hits in the process of initiating an attack as long as he can get on top of his victim quickly in order to do the maximum amount of damage. He won't be concerned about points or judges or whether or not he is following the rules—he will only be thinking about how much damage he can do.

In a real fight, there are no weight divisions, there are no preset rules, there's no crowd cheering or jeering, and there are certainly no prizes either for the first or second place. Because a real fight can come out of nowhere, your adrenaline is pumping; you lose the use of your fine motor skills (which allow you to do all those lovely fancy things that you practised every night perfectly in class) and everything comes down essentially to the basic instinct to survive. Because of that basic need for survival, there is no guarantee that the fight will be barehanded. More often than not, there is someone with some kind of weapon attacking someone who is unarmed, and there is often a lot of flailing around and uncoordinated movements because nothing is ever pretty in a real fight.

You may be reading this and saying to yourself that what I have said is completely wrong and that you have seen two guys face off and duke it out while surrounded by onlookers etc. Well, this is not a real fight. Believe it or not, this type of fight has rules where at some stage someone will jump in and end it. I believe a term was coined for this phenomenon by a man named Keith R. Kernspecht[4] (grand master of WingTsun). He called it ritual combat—where two opponents face off both knowing that the fight was about to happen and allowing the other some measure of time to realise that the fight was about to happen and get ready and calm his/her nerves. This is not a true fight; as I mentioned before it is a spectacle. Even though there may be animosity between the two fighters, it cannot

---

[4]   Grand Master Keith R. Kernspecht has written many books over the years relating to the martial arts, two of which are called *On Single Combat* and *Blitz Defence: Your strategy against thugs.* Very much worth reading if you're serious about broadening your horizons.

be a true test of their ill will towards one another because it is a controlled environment, and a measure of calm is maintained with the knowledge that if things get too bad for one of the fighters there will be someone to step in and stop the confrontation.

When a real fight occurs, it will be almost totally random. You could have been out with your friends and seen a movie, had a couple of drinks, you could be laughing and yelling and be as happy as you've ever been in your life and then all of a sudden it's on. You're in your favourite jeans that are a little too restrictive to throw kicks in; plus you have your phone, keys, and wallet in your pocket. You've got your favourite gold chain around your neck and your best shirt and shoes on, your hair's done nicely, and you are simply not the same person who goes to class three nights a week and smashes everyone in sparring. You're not in the mood for a fight and all of your favourite moves cannot be done because of the restrictions of your clothing. Sounds infuriating, doesn't it? Well, fights are annoying and almost always happen when you don't want them to, unless, of course, you go out looking for one.

I feel that I must also point out the phenomenon known as an adrenaline dump. It is a basic physiological reaction that we have retained from our 'caveman' days in which whenever something traumatic is happening and we think we are in immediate danger our body pumps adrenaline through our system, making us faster and stronger for a short period of time so we can extract ourselves from the encounter. Its drawbacks, however, are the temporary diminishment of higher brain function which causes us to react to rather than think about the situation we find ourselves in and also, as mentioned before, our fine motor skills diminish, and we are only left with our basic movements which rules out a lot of the technical moves that we find ourselves learning in the martial arts. Obviously, this is all from the victim's point of view as an attacker will know what is about to happen and will essentially be a lot calmer in the situation unless something unexpected occurs such as the victim fighting back effectively. If you have never experienced an adrenaline dump, then it will be quite a shock when it first occurs, and you will find yourself somewhat exhausted after a short period when the adrenaline wears off (another down point).

Apart from the obvious physiological aspects of fighting, there is really nothing scientific about it in my opinion; it should not be broken down, analysed, and confused with an academic pursuit. Too many highly skilled people have tried to turn martial arts into something scholarly, for example, what to do with an alpha male and how to approach the situation in a calm and collected manner but still maintain an air of authority. These are not things that you can train for as it all boils down to what kind of person you are. If you try and train yourself to be more assertive without actually having the proper attitude to back it up, then you come across as fake, and many thugs will see straight through you. These 'scientists of the martial arts' have turned survival into something that has right and wrong answers, but what they are mainly doing is trying to humanise something that is a basic animal instinct—and this causes many people to think way too much when they should just be reacting. Many people are now overly concerned about the legality of defending themselves, and this causes hesitation and hesitation causes openings which can be exploited. I've always lived by the philosophy of *live today, worry tomorrow*, and if a fight came out of nowhere and you are defending yourself, then you have little to worry about. If you provoked the fight, however, you may not only find yourself in some legal trouble, but you're also an idiot. Your personality and your martial training will determine how you fare in violent or potentially violent situations. If your mind is too clouded with academic or psychological babble, then your reaction time is going to be much slower than normal, and this could cause a great deal of problems when you're in the middle of an altercation. If you want to avoid a fight (obviously, you can't avoid one that you don't know is coming, but say for instance you think there might be a fight brewing), then all you have to do is let go of your ego, bow down, and be absolutely passive towards the person. Beg if it will get you out of the situation. Believe me though, it's harder than it sounds to let go of your ego once you've been challenged, particularly if you're not used to people disrespecting you.

The absolute reality of close quarter combat and self-defence is that if someone really wants to cause you harm, then he/she is going to achieve that by any means possible, and most times you will never even see it coming—much like my friend Dale. He was highly trained and very skilled, and I have no doubt in my mind whatsoever that if they had been a metre or so apart and that fellow had tried to hit him, Dale would have turned him into chopped meat.

Gentlemanly fights are very rare these days, and we can no longer settle our disputes 'outside' and have a drink together afterwards. Society has become vicious and cowardly, and there is no way to reverse the damage that has been done. These days you will be sucker-punched from behind, and then your attacker and his friends will kick you while you're on the ground. Either that or perhaps the person you are fighting will be a super-angry drugged-up steroid freak who has an incredibly high pain threshold and no regard for human welfare. No matter how hard you think you are, there is always going to be someone harder around the corner or behind you. I know people who train every day to withstand pain to a degree where you cannot hurt them by conventional fighting methods. A kick to the stomach will only make them angrier and a punch to the nose will make them laugh. That's not to say that they are awesome fighters; it's just a matter of fact that they can withstand all but the strongest hits, and more often than not, you will have to attack the weak spots (groin, throat, eyes, etc.) to do any damage to them.

The best example of this type of person that I can think of is a man by the name of Lenny McLean. Many of you might know Lenny from his appearances in movies like *Lock, Stock and Two Smoking Barrels* where he played an enforcer. In real life, Lenny was an unbeaten bare-knuckle no-rules fighter who earned his living with his body. He was stabbed and shot multiple times and was a self-confessed 'lunatic' when it came to fighting. He wasn't scared to fight anyone, and the amount of punishment he took during his fights for both money and necessity was unbelievable. I recommend his autobiography *The Guv'nor*[5] to anyone seriously interested in furthering their knowledge of fighting as not only does it have some valuable insight into fighting, but it's also a really good read.

With Lenny in mind, I would now like to talk a little about your mindset and how it impacts on your ability to defend yourself in a real situation. As mentioned above, Lenny was a self-confessed 'lunatic', and although he was actually a lovely man (as long as you were on his good side), he would be ready to snap at a moment's notice. It was simply his personality—he was always ready for a fight. However, just think about this for a minute. Are you always ready for a fight? Can you deliver punishment at a moment's notice or do you need a few seconds to both mentally and physically prepare yourself? I can honestly say that I can't just fire off at will because I still feel the shock, and it takes me a few seconds to get my head around what's happening. Sure I can defend myself on a basic level if an attack comes from the front, but I'm not so alert as to be able to intercept an attack from the side or rear, especially if I'm occupied by something like a conversation etc. This is important stuff to think about and something that many people do not learn until it is too late. Take, for example, the

---

5   Lenny McLean and Peter Gerrard, 1998, *The Guv'nor*, (Bookmarque: Croydon, Surrey, Great Britain).

fact that when you go to training you know that at some point in the night you are going to be defending against attacks and you are going to be doing various drills and so forth, and as a consequence, you prepare yourself for the physical exertion to come. However, with reference to a scenario I mentioned earlier, you might be out with your friends or family and having a great time and fighting would probably be the absolute last thing on your mind, when all of a sudden you find yourself in a violent encounter, and trust me, it always plays a little on your nerves.

Now I'm not trying to say that you need to be like Lenny McLean and be constantly ready to brawl, but what I suggest is more along the lines of situational awareness or basic common sense. Learn to read the signs; don't stand or pass near obviously aggravated people, and keep your wits about you when in crowds or strange/dark places. By using basic common sense and a little situational awareness, you can avoid a fight altogether or at least increase your chances of being ready for it or seeing it coming.

Going back to the idea of striking vital areas, one has to consider that there is a reason that these moves are banned in pretty much all combat sports due to the fact that they are moves designed to *end fights* and they are illegal because they take all of the 'sport' out of the fight. A hard shin to the groin is going to crush certain parts on males and do some pretty serious damage to females; a strike to the throat or neck is going to at the very least disorientate an attacker and at most it will kill them. Head-butts and shots to the knees/ears/eyes are all savage attacks and as such work to create maximum impact with minimum effort, and it is a simple fact that people in industries such as military, security, and government agencies who need realistic self-defence training are being taught to strike these areas.

One last subject I would like to talk about is the all-in brawl. Let's say, for example, that you are out with a group of friends and you come up against a group of equal size (which almost never happens), and a fight breaks out. These are always messy and are pretty much 'every man for himself' types of affairs in which attackers come from all sides at the same time, and technique, for the most part, goes out the window. You are going to get hit if you don't get out, and sometimes those hits come from friends who are swinging blindly into the maelstrom of bodies. If weapons are involved, the chances are good that someone might die, and if you're a wrestler and you take someone to the ground, you are putting yourself in even more danger. If you can't stay out of it, you need to stay on your feet, you need to keep your hands up, and you need to be brutal. Almost all of the big brawls I've seen have been ended by police armed with pepper spray and batons; they just spray the entire mob, and when they are all screaming, the police move in with batons drawn until they lie on the ground. I've seen a lucky few manage to get out of the brawl before this happens and get away, but most end up having a bad night. Nobody's a winner in fights like these.

My Experiences

Now I would like to share some stories with you in an attempt to convey just how I formed my opinions about the realities of fighting. I'm not going to tell you about every single scenario I've ever been in, but I *am* going to convey the more important fights that have shaped my attitude towards fighting—and why you should avoid a fight at all costs. The stories are based on actual events, and I was either directly involved or was an eye witness to them. Hopefully, they might help to dispel any illusions you have about real fighting.

Sucker-punched

I was walking down a somewhat empty street one day when I noticed a man leaning against a wall, looking as though he was hurt. I was walking towards him when he looked up directly at me, and as I got closer and asked him if he was okay, he hit me in the mouth with a fast, wild punch which sent me back a few steps with both pain and shock.

'I want your fucking money,' he said to me.

'No, mate,' was my reply.

He moved towards me, and we grabbed each other by the shirt. The altercation ended after I continuously kicked him in the groin (roughly half a dozen times), and he fell down, letting out a terrible moaning noise as I quickly walked off in case he had a weapon. Simple, effective, and to the point.

Wayne Went Crazy

My friend Wayne has always been a bit of a scary guy. He wasn't overly aggressive, mind you, but he was just one of those people who had something dark inside them waiting for an opportunity to present itself so that it could unleash the devil. The day I finally saw him erupt was one of the most horrible things I'd ever seen. His son came inside while we were watching a movie, and the poor kid was covered in blood. He'd been attacked by a group of young men who were wandering the street and decided to steal his wallet and shoes. Wayne, taking a moment to look over his son's injuries, then proceeded to grab a two-foot-long metal pole from his shed and took off down the street—completely ignoring my pleas to call the police rather than deal with it himself. The only thing I could do was chase after him and watch as he slowed to a walk and approached the five well-built young men. As he came towards them, they stood and swore at him, and by the time they realised he was armed it was too late. It seemed as if everyone but Wayne had gone into slow motion. Obviously, it was my brain playing tricks on me as I realised that Wayne wasn't going to waste time talking and posing. He was seeing red and I was frozen. With a series of incredibly fast hits, Wayne knocked them all to the ground and then went to work on the ringleader, repeatedly and mercilessly bludgeoning him with the pole. I realised that Wayne needed to be stopped, so I tackled him, rugby style, to the ground where he tried to attack me until he came to his senses and calmed down. Luckily, none of the blokes were killed or too severely injured, and Wayne managed to get off without any prison time. Maybe he went a bit overboard, but they deserved it in my opinion.

Old School Bar

I was on holiday and went back to Sydney to see all of my friends from school. At school, we had been a tight unit. We weren't popular or overly academic or anything like that; we were just average kids who looked after each other and watched each other's backs in a tough environment. We were good friends. On my first night back, we went out at night to one of the city's hot spots. The night was a lot of fun until we ran into another group of guys who used to go to our school. It was unbelievable; those guys had not changed at all and were still the same jerks that they had always been and acted just as aggressive towards us as they always did, which led to problems. A fight broke out, and I was standing there dumbfounded. I could not believe that those fools were still acting the way they did when we were kids; not only that, but they actually started a brawl with us in a pub. I kept standing there stupidly until I noticed one of them attacking Mick—the smallest, sweetest, most harmless guy in our group. The main thing that made me angry about that was the fact that Mick was deliberately trying to stay out of the way of the fight, and that coward attacked him anyway. That guy had long hair, so it was easy enough to grab him by the back of his hair, pull backwards, and smash his nose in with two hits to the face. After that, it was time to run because the bouncers were coming and they were all very big men with no visible necks. I'm a good fighter, but I'm not stupid and besides the bouncers were just doing their job. Mick and I got out of there straight away and went home.

Bikers

I was working as a bouncer in the town's most popular club at the time and people from all walks of life came to this club, including members of the local motorcycle club. They weren't as bad as everyone made them out to be because the last thing they wanted was to do something illegal and get into some kind of trouble in public. However, if they were pushed somehow, they did not hesitate in throwing down. Most people do not understand that most members of biker clubs have been involved with violence ever since they were kids, and often those groups have a 'blood in, blood out' policy where you have to literally fight to get in *and* out of the club. They are mostly experienced street fighters and they have no interest in fighting fair. They're all about maximum damage with minimum effort and risk to themselves. I actually became quite friendly with most of them because it's much easier knowing that the toughest guys in the pub are on your side—and it also makes it easier to deal with them when they get out of hand.

One night, three of the boys were standing at the bar having a drink, and a stupid girl (you know the type—short skirt—thinking everyone finds her as appealing as she finds herself) went up to them and demanded that they buy her a drink. When they refused, she slapped one of them and he slapped her back. From there, everything went pear shaped. A fellow standing off to the side turned around just in time to see the girl get slapped and incorrectly assumed that the biker had hit her for no reason. His response was to smash a glass over the biker's head—which caused all three of the boys to set upon him. Now in the movies and in a lot of people's minds when someone is attacked by a group of people, it is usually a one after the other affair. This is never the case in my experience. All three of them latched on to this guy at the same time, belting him across the head until he collapsed on the floor at which time they started kicking and stomping him until we pulled them away from him. The young bloke was unconscious and bleeding from absolutely everywhere (mouth, nose, ears, eyes). The entire altercation lasted no more than ten seconds.

Drug Traffickers

Drugs are horrible, evil bloody things and they ruin lives, and a lot of the time, the people that traffic them are just as twisted. I was working at the door of a local nightclub as a bouncer and I noticed these three guys walk out. We'd had our eyes on them the entire night because we knew that they were trafficking 'ice' (a new form of drug) to our town from one of the major cities not far away and that they were up to no good in our club. They were good at what they did though, and we couldn't catch them doing anything illegal, and there was really no valid reason to remove them from the premises.

As I watched them leave the club, I noticed them whispering to each other as they approached an intoxicated person who was standing in the street and having a cigarette. One of the three men walked up to the guy and started talking to him while the other two seemed to ignore him and walked past only to turn around and come up behind the guy without him even knowing that they were there. I knew something was happening, and just as I called for someone to cover the door for me, they attacked him.

It was actually quite amazing to watch (although it was a horrible thing to happen) as those three guys attacked the drunk fellow at the exact same moment, smashing him about the head with punches and then booting him in the head repeatedly until they noticed me sprinting at them. They managed to get away, but their victim looked like something out of a cartoon—missing teeth, big welts protruding from his face, and blood everywhere, all from an attack that lasted three seconds. He survived and the police were able to catch the three men who attacked him, and again I was taught another lesson about street attacks.

Revenge of the Nerd

I remember there was a little watering hole that my friends and I liked to go to during the week if we had nothing to do or were bored or something like that, and after a while, we began to find ourselves there just about every day, playing pool or just having a quiet drink or whatnot. We weren't the only regulars though, and like most places that serve alcohol, there were drunken idiots around. This one particular fellow was a very large guy, easily six and a half feet tall, but he was a complete coward and had no interest in picking on anyone who could even be a remote threat to him. He talked a big game but had absolutely nothing to back it up.

However, there was one night when he must have decided to show everyone how tough he was and he was on the hunt for a fight. Unfortunately, the first one to catch his eye was a small, thin, pale-looking kid who I guessed as being barely eighteen.

'What are you fucking looking at, dickhead?' The challenge was issued and it was clear the kid was in trouble, but instead of shrinking away and looking down, the kid stood up from his chair. Bad move. The big guy took this as a challenge and had the kid on the ground in a matter of seconds, smashing him in the ribs with punches until the big guy's friends pulled him off and dragged him out of the pub. By the time my friends and I realised that the kid couldn't fight back and made our way across the pub from the poolroom, the kid had managed to sit up, but he was crying, embarrassed and bleeding from the nose. When we asked him if he needed a hand, he didn't speak to us; he just let us pick him up and then he hobbled out of the pub. Poor bugger!

For a couple of weeks, we debated whether or not we should try and sort out this big bloke (who kept coming back to the pub every day like he'd done nothing wrong and why on earth the owners allowed him back in was beyond me), but we realised that if we tried to do anything to him we would have a problem with his friends (who we didn't have anything against), and it would simply cause too much undue stress for the publican if a massive brawl broke out. Our hands were tied, and to be completely honest, it really was none of our business and the last thing we wanted was to make more trouble for the owners and staff at the pub. It wasn't until about a month later that something happened to the big guy, and nobody expected it to happen the way it did.

Apparently the kid who had been beaten up a month before had been waiting, every night it seems, for the big guy to leave the pub alone so he could carry out his own form of justice. The night it happened was almost pitch black and while the big guy crossed the parking lot alone after a few drinks. The only reason that we know it was the kid was because after all of the screaming we ran outside and saw him running away down the road with a cricket bat in his hand. We found the big guy unconscious in the parking lot covered in blood and called an ambulance. We later found out that he had a broken leg, two broken arms (probably from trying to defend himself), as well many other injuries.

Perhaps the most beautiful thing about it was that none of us knew who the kid was, and we never saw him again, and although it was a brutal and probably a criminal act that he'd committed none of us, including the guy's friends, could really blame him. He'd gotten what he'd deserved in our opinion. The kid didn't deserve to get beaten up like he had as he had been just trying to have a quiet drink and was attacked for no reason by this big coward. It made me feel a bit better too, knowing that he hadn't gotten away with what he'd done to the kid.

The Beatdown

The following is a rather embarrassing and painful moment in my life, where I learned the cost of complacency of both body and mind. I was not in a very good place in my life at the time and it was, I believe, the main contributor to my not being able to defend myself effectively during the incident I am about to describe.

I had not trained for six months in any way, shape or form, and it was obvious. I had gained some weight and generally did not look healthy at all. I had been having some personal issues and some problems with work at the time and my head was just genuinely not on the task when I was at work one night. I was working security at one of the worst shitholes in town and there were only two of us in the whole place. Every night there were scumbags that had to be dealt with and the environment was simply not safe at all.

This particular night there was a fight between two large groups of youths out in the back car park and one of those groups was just trying to get away where the other was the more aggressive. Now, what happened next was quite strange and my memory of it was a little clouded because I ended up with a slight head injury but what I do remember comes back to me from time to time when I'm daydreaming and I'm confused by it every time.

I ran into the middle of the group and pushed a few of the fighters away from each other, yelling at them to go home and while some members of the group being attacked decided that this was their time to escape, there were some of the others that were too busy fighting to listen to me. After my interruption of the fight, some of the more aggressive group now had their sights set on me for some reason and while I was screaming down the radio (we wore radios to keep in touch with each other) for my partner to come and help me, about seven or eight males from the more aggressive group launched themselves at me. Unlike in the movies when a group attacks you, they all came at once. I had been in situations similar to this before so I should have had an idea of what to do.

However, and this is the part that I keep reliving, instead of defending myself I just stood there and watched them strike me. I blocked a few punches and then covered up and let their blows come at me. None of the punches were particularly hard and I didn't fall down but I covered up and just waited. Out of the corner of my eye I saw my partner run out of the pub and jump on one of the guys that was attacking me and in turn one of the others tried to attack him. Finally, I moved and tackled the young male who was attempting to hurt my partner but once I was on the ground the group was on me again and I just covered up while being kicked and punched. After about a minute the police turned up and arrests were made and I stood there dumbfounded at what had happened. A friend came to pick me up and took me to the hospital where I was told I had a mild concussion but that was not the main thing that was worrying me.

For months I tried to make sense of why I didn't react like usual. Some people tried to tell me that it was because I hadn't trained in awhile but in the end I think it all came down to my mindset. I think I simply did not want to fight anymore and just gave up rather than having to defend myself. I had some time off after the incident in order to get my head straight and I started training again, but I have never been able to shake that feeling of helplessness that I had that night. I suppose you could say that it haunts me a little. I've never had the same thing happen in years since and I've been in similar situations where my 'fight instinct' has kicked in straight away—even though I don't really end up on the winning side when I'm being attacked by more than one person at a time.

My little story here really goes to show how your mindset can play a factor in how effectively or ineffectively you can defend yourself. I was in a frame of mind where I was not able to do my job effectively and it could have cost me a lot more than a mild concussion. These days, I strongly believe that sometimes those who are trained to fight are not always ready to fight and I have had the discussion with many of my friends and most of them seem to agree that good training and situational awareness will help you defend yourself but can only do so much. You can never be ready a hundred percent of the time and when your mind is elsewhere and trouble starts your training is not always going to kick in when it is most needed. Try and figure out what kind of person you are and you may be more effectively able to get yourself out of bad situations or at least understand how you are going to react if a certain situation occurs.

Laurie and the Bar Stool

Again, one night at work, my friend Laurie and two other guards were embroiled in a fight in the main bar of a popular club. After a minute or so, more guards appeared and the aggressive patrons were subdued on the ground. However, one of those people's friends was not happy with the treatment of his friends and picked up a heavy wooden bar stool and swung it as hard as he could at Laurie's head. Laurie was on his knees at the time helping to subdue one of the aggressive patrons and did not see the stool coming, and had it not been for one of our other co-workers sticking his arm in the way and cutting down the impact of the blow, Laurie would have certainly been killed. As it turned out, the blow was hard enough to give him brain damage, and to this day, Laurie is living off work compensation and his prospects for the future are dim at best—all because some idiot did not understand the impact of his actions. Unfortunately, this is the type of immature, irresponsible moron that modern society is creating by the truckload. From what I remember, the attacker didn't even get close to the punishment he deserved.

Lost Eye

This final story is a recollection of the worst injury I have ever seen in a violent scenario, and it's one of the main reasons that I removed myself from the violent nightclub scene. I was watching an argument between two guys, which was quickly becoming heated, and I decided that it was time to do my job and move them along so that a fight didn't break out. I didn't get there in time. As the verbal argument between the two young men reached its height, one of the guys smashed a glass into the face of the other and a piece of the glass cut the poor fellow's eye into half. That was the entire altercation, but it is something that the victim will remember for the rest of his life due to the fact that he now has a fake eye. Obviously, the attacker was caught and given a prison sentence of a couple of years, but it hardly seems fair compared with the fact that the victim's life has been changed so drastically. This is something that could happen to any of us in any altercation that we're involved in, and it is why I constantly stress the point to my students that avoiding a fight and staying out of the way is the most sensible choice you can make. It was also the most disgusting thing that I have ever seen, and the screams from the victim will remain in my mind forever, I think.

Bye-Bye, Boys and Girls

Hopefully something within these pages has had some positive effect on you as you have read them either as a martial artist or as just a person. It is my hope that I have somehow opened your eyes to the facts of the martial arts and the realities that go hand in hand with them. I hope also that you will now attempt to learn and research as much as you can as it was not my intention throughout this book to preach but more to act as a starting block from which you may base your new outlook on martial arts and fighting.

From these few stories that I have recounted, there are some common elements that you may have noticed. Real fights are always fast, vicious, and unpredictable. You very rarely get the chance to square off like in sport or in the movies, and the person who wins is always the one who can do the most damage in the shortest amount of time, usually by hitting the other person somewhat off guard.

The aim of these stories, in fact, the entire book, was not to glorify violence in any way, and hopefully as you read them you realised just how easy it can be to get hurt. The practice of martial arts is good in so many ways and for many it is a way of life, but you must always remember the ultimate truth. Nobody is invincible.

Index

K

Kanarek, Mike Lee   24
karate   15
katana   32
Kernspecht, Keith R.   37
Krav Maga   19, 34
kung fu   14

L

Laurie   52
Lee, Bruce   17

M

martial arts:
  aspects of   13
  evolution of   14-15
  guideline for a student of   12
  learning   21-5
  mainstream   19
  military   19, 34
  mixed   18-19
  oriental   14
  spirituality in   13
  teaching   27
  training in   28-31
  weapons in   32-5
McDojos   27
McLean, Lenny   40-1
MCMAP (Marine Corps Martial Arts
    Program)   19
Mick   45
MMA (mixed martial arts) *see* martial
    arts, mixed

N

ninjutsu   35
Norris, Chuck   36
nunchaku   32

O

Okinawa, Japan   15

R

ritual combat   37
Roger   25

S

Sambo   19
samurai   13
self-defence   26, 34, 36, 39
Shaolin Buddhist monks   13
Shaolin Temple   14-15
solo training   30 *see also* martial arts,
    training in
spirituality   13, 19, 22

T

Tae Kwon Do   23

V

violence   7

W

Wayne   44
Wing Chun Kung Fu   16

Edwards Brothers Malloy
Thorofare, NJ USA
April 30, 2014